Contents

The history of speed

People have always wanted to travel faster. First, they went faster by riding a camel or a horse. Then they used horses to pull carriages with wheels. People also loaded cargoes on to boats and used the power of the wind to travel across the sea.

People can reach speeds of nearly 70km/h on horseback

Clipper ships sailed across the seas powered by wind.

Then **steam power** was invented and used to run the first steam trains.

Stephenson's *Rocket* reached 47km/h at its launch in 1829.

Next the motor car was designed, with its **internal combustion engine**. Karl Benz's **automobile** of 1893 only reached 17km/h, but after that cars got faster. Finally the aeroplane was developed, and then space travel.

Karl Benz and his daughter Clara in 1893.

5

World speed records

People keep trying to break the world speed records for travelling on land and water, and through the air.

In 1964 the British driver Donald Campbell broke both land and water world records. He set the water record at 444km/h in his boat *Bluebird K7*, and the land record at 690km/h in his car *Bluebird CN7*. Campbell was killed in 1967, travelling at more than 480km/h on Lake Coniston, England.

More recently, in 1997, the British driver Richard Noble broke the land speed record and the **sound barrier** by driving at 1,228km/h in his jet-propelled *Thrust SSC*. A jet-propelled car is one that has a **jet engine**.

The British-built *Thrust SSC*.
SSC stands for supersonic car.

The US airforce *SR-71* last flew in 1999.
Thrust and *SR-71* are very similar in shape.

Ken Warby from Australia set a new world water speed record in 1978, zooming along at 511km/h in a jet-powered **hydroplane**.

The flight speed record is held by American pilot Eldon Joersz, who in 1976 flew the jet-powered *SR-71 Blackbird* at 3,326km/h – 3.3 times the speed of sound.

On rails
The world train speed record was set in 2007 by the French **TGV** which sped along at 574km/h.

Motor racing

Formula 1, or F1, is the top class of motor racing. The 'formula' is a set of rules which all competitors must follow.

The F1 races are called **Grands Prix**. They are usually held on special tracks, but are sometimes run on streets that have been closed to the public.

Prizewinners
At the end of the F1 season there are two prizes, one for the best driver and one for the maker of the winning car.

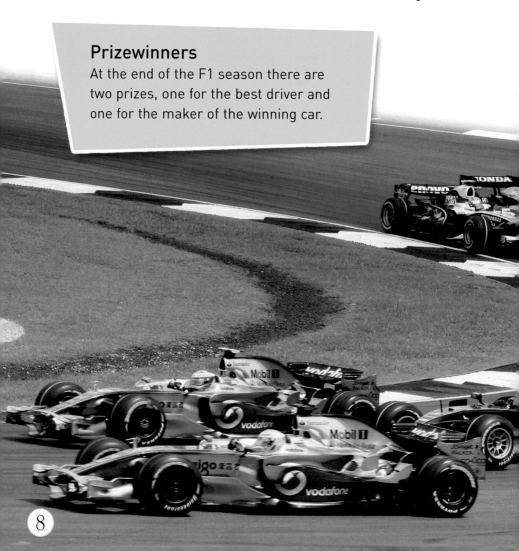

KINGFISHER READERS

level 5

Record Breakers-
The Fastest

Brenda Stones

KINGFISHER

 KINGFISHER

First published 2012 by Kingfisher
an imprint of Macmillan Children's Books
a division of Macmillan Publishers Limited
20 New Wharf Road, London N1 9RR
Basingstoke and Oxford
Associated companies throughout the world
www.panmacmillan.com

Series editor: Heather Morris
Literacy consultant: Hilary Horton

ISBN: 978-0-7534-3066-8
Copyright © Macmillan Publishers Ltd 2012

9 8 7 6 5 4 3 2 1

1TR/1011/WKT/UNTD/105MA

A CIP catalogue record for this book is available from the British Library.

Printed in China

Picture credits

The Publisher would like to thank the following for permission to reproduce their material. Every care has been
taken to trace copyright holders. However, if there have been unintentional omissions or failure to trace copyright
holders, we apologize and will, if informed, endeavour to make corrections in any future edition
(t = top, b = bottom, c = centre, r = right, l = left):
Cover Corbis/Larry W. Smith/epa, Corbis/Dean Lewis, Corbis/Bettman, NaturePL/Dave Watts;
Pages 4tl Alamy/Juniors Bildarchiv; 5br Corbis/Bettmann; 7b Alamy/Tom Craig; 8 Corbis/Stephane Cardinale;
9 Corbis/Schlegelmilch; 10b Corbis/Dean Lewis; 11t Alamy/www.gerardbrown.co.uk; 11b Shutterstock (SS)/Jacek
Chabraszewski; 12 Corbis/Bettman; 13tl Corbis/Stephen Hird/Reuters; 13c Corbis/Stephen Hird/Reuters; 14cl Corbis/
Michael Nicholson; 16 Getty/UMA/PCN; 17 Getty/Sung-Jin Kang; 18c Corbis/Gopal Chitrakar/Reuters; 18–19 SS/
Dimtry Pichungin; 20cr Getty/MLB Photo Archive; 20bl Getty/Lakruwan Wanniarachch/Reuters; 21 Getty/Patrick
Kovarik/AFP; 22 Getty/AFP; 23tl Getty/Bloomberg; 23cr Corbis/Larry W. Smith/epa; 24 Corbis/Olivier Maire/epa;
25t SS/Jonathan Larson; 25b Corbis/Xu Jiajun/Xinghua; 26 Frank Lane Picture Agency (FLPA)/Fritz Polking; 29t FLPA/
Willi Rolfes/Minden; 29b SS/Sebastian Knight; 31c NaturePL/Brandon Cole; 31b NaturePL/ Wild wonders of Europe/
Zankl; 34l, 34c & 34r NaturePL/Dave Watts; 35 Science Photo Library/Harvard College Observatory; 36 SS/SergeyIT;
38 Corbis/Hannibal Hanschke; 39t Getty/Anwar Hussein; 39b Getty/Dan Kitwood; 40 SS/agophoto; 41 SS/Jeremy
Richards; 42c Corbis/Shannon Stapleton/Reuters; 42b Corbis/Enrique de la Osa/Reuters; 43t Corbis/Esa
Alexander/Reuters; 43b Corbis/Murad Sezer/Reuters; 44tl SS/Nikonov; 44bl SS/Peter Wollinga;
44br SS/Studio37; 45 Getty/Mario Tama. All other images Kingfisher Artbank.

How do you win at Formula 1?
One of the trickiest tactics in the race is overtaking. This is the only way you can get past your competitors.

The cars race at speeds of up to 386km/h, powered by engines which turn at 18,000 **revs** per minute. The cars go faster because of their **aerodynamic** shape, the **suspension**, and the strength of the tyres.

Pedal power

People want to travel as fast as they can on bicycles, too! One of the earliest bicycles was the **penny farthing**, invented in 1871. This was the first bicycle to have tyres made of rubber. Its first speed record was just 25.5km/h.

This bicycle was named after two coins of different sizes, the penny and the farthing.

Today bicycles go pretty fast. At the Olympic Games in 1992, British cyclist Chris Boardman won a gold medal at a top speed of 52km/h. He was riding a **carbon fibre** bicycle designed by Lotus.

In 2007 another British cyclist, Chris Hoy, set a world record for the 500 metre flying start, at 24.758 seconds.

Matthew Crampton, Chris Hoy and Jason Kenny, racing in 2007's World Cup in Sydney, Australia

A recumbent has a more comfortable seat and handlebars than a racing bike.

In the 1970s a new design of **recumbent** bicycle appeared. The rider pedals lying down, so there is less **wind resistance**.

How fast are you on a bicycle?
Time yourself riding over a fixed distance, and see if you can improve your speed. What makes you go faster?

Fastest transport on water

There are all kinds of speed records for boats. The Blue Riband is an award for the fastest passenger liner to cross the Atlantic. This record has been held by the SS *United States* since 1952.

The SS *United States* set the speed record for sailing both eastwards and westwards.

There have been plenty of records set by sailing boats. In 1967 the British sailor Francis Chichester became the first person to sail **solo** around the world, taking 9 months, 1 day.

Ellen MacArthur's boat *Castorama* was specially designed for her as she is only 1.57m tall.

Since then, the technology of sailing boats has improved immensely. In 2001 Ellen MacArthur, from Great Britain, became the first woman and the youngest person to sail solo around the world. Then in 2005 she set a world record of 71 days, 14 hours, 18 minutes, 33 seconds. This was broken in 2008 by the French sailor Francis Joyon, who cut 14 days off MacArthur's time.

Did you know?
Sailing around the world westwards takes twice as long as sailing around eastwards, because the tides and winds slow you down.

Fastest in air and space

The Wright brothers made the first successful powered flight in 1903. Their plane only just cleared the ground, travelling at a speed of 10.9km/h.

 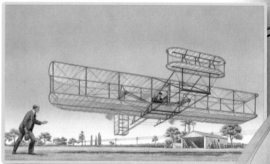

American brothers Wilbur and Orville Wright made their first successful flight in a biplane called the *Flyer* (above).

The first solo flight across the Atlantic was made by the American Charles Lindbergh in 1927 and took 33.5 hours. By 2003 *Concorde* could cross the Atlantic in 2 hours, 52 minutes, 59 seconds.

Cruising at speed
Concorde's average cruising speed was 2,140km/h, nearly twice the speed of sound.

Voyager 1 flew past both Saturn
and Jupiter, taking photos.

To leave the **atmosphere** and fly into space, a
spacecraft has to travel much faster than an ordinary
aeroplane. The fastest manned vehicle in space was
Apollo 10, which reached 38,896km/h in 1969.

In 1977, *Voyager 1*, an unmanned spacecraft, flew
at 61,722km/h.

The fastest man-made object in space was *Helios 2*,
sent to study the Sun in 1976. It flew at 252,792km/h
and reached the Sun in three months.

Running and swimming

Running is the fastest way we can move on land without using any form of transport. When we talk about 'the fastest man on Earth' this usually means the best sprinter over a short distance. Today the fastest man on Earth is the Jamaican Usain Bolt, who set world records of 9.58 seconds over 100 metres and 19.19 seconds over 200 metres in 2009.

Bolt at the 2009 World Athletics Championships in Berlin, Germany

Ian Thorpe set 18 individual world records between 1999 and 2002. He retired from swimming at the age of 24, but in 2011 started training again, ready for the 2012 Olympics.

The Australian Ian Thorpe, 'the Thorpedo', holds the record for being the fastest 14-year-old in the history of swimming. In 1998, aged 15, he became the youngest ever world champion when he won the 400 metres **freestyle** in Perth, Australia.

Which is the fastest stroke?

1 front crawl: 2.387 metres per second
2 butterfly: 2.177 metres per second
3 backstroke: 2.043 metres per second
4 breaststroke: 1.839 metres per second

Climbing and falling

Some people run up mountains. The American climber Sean Burch ran up Mount Kilimanjaro in Africa in a record 5 hours, 28 minutes, 48 seconds!

The record speed for climbing Mount Everest, the world's highest mountain, is also impressive. In 2004, Nepalese climber Pemba Dorje Sherpa climbed from base camp to the summit in 8 hours, 10 minutes, breaking the record held by Lakpa Gelu Sherpa by 2 hours.

Pemba Dorje Sherpa

Joseph Kittinger just after he jumped out of the balloon

Can you imagine **free-falling** in space? In 1960 the American pilot Joseph Kittinger broke all the records. He jumped out of a balloon and fell for 4 minutes, 36 seconds, reaching a speed of 988km/h, before opening his parachute at 5,500 metres. This was the fastest a human had ever travelled through the atmosphere.

The summit of Mount Everest, 8,848 metres high

Fastest ball games

What is the fastest baseball pitch ever thrown? The record is 162.3km/h, set by the American player Lynn Nolan Ryan playing for the California Angels team in 1974.

The fastest ball ever bowled in cricket was by Shoaib Akhtar of Pakistan in 2003. The ball travelled at 161.3km/h.

Akhtar is nicknamed 'the Rawalpindi Express' after his home town.

Tennis players hit the ball with a racket to make it travel faster. The Croatian player Ivo Karlovic holds the world record for the fastest tennis serve. In 2011 he served a ball at 251km/h. The women's record for the fastest serve is held by the American player Venus Williams. In 2007 she served a ball at 208km/h.

Lynn Nolan Ryan throwing a fast baseball pitch, this time for the Texas Rangers

Venus Williams serves in the French Open Championship in May 2010.

Fastest scoring

The International Federation of Association Football (FIFA) lists the footballers who scored the fastest goals ever in World Cup games.

Fastest goal after kick-off: Hakan Sükür of Turkey in 11 seconds (2002).

Fastest goal in a final: Johan Neeskens of the Netherlands in 90 seconds (1974).

Fastest football hat trick: László Kiss of Hungary in 8 minutes (1982).

Fastest sending off: José Batista of Uruguay after 56 seconds (1986).

Neeskens' rapid goal was scored with a penalty kick after less than 2 minutes of play.

Jay Culter (left), the fastest passer in American football

Devin Hester (above) made an amazingly fast touchdown in Miami in 2007, but his team still lost the match.

Here are some records for American Football's Super Bowl championship.

Fastest touchdown from start: Devin Hester of the Chicago Bears in 14 seconds.

Fastest field goal: Tony Franklin of the New England Patriots in 1 minute, 19 seconds.

Fastest pass by a quarterback: 101km/h by Jay Cutler of the Chicago Bears in 2007.

Fastest NFL team to get to the Super Bowl: the Kansas City Chiefs began in 1960 and played in their first Super Bowl in 1967.

Speedy winter sports

Why do we move fast on skates and skis? The simple answer is that as the skis press down on snow or ice, they make a film of water. This reduces **friction** so you slide faster.

Speed skiers have helmets to protect their heads and foam pads to protect their legs.

In speed skating, the average speed rose from 45 to 52km/h from 1971 to 2009. The world speed record for skiing downhill is 251.4km/h, set by Simone Origone of Italy in 2006.

In Canada this sport is called bobsled. Here the Canadian team race towards a 2006 Olympic silver medal.

Bobsleighs are made of steel on the outside, and carbon fibre on the inside. They are designed to reduce friction. Racers wear spiked running shoes to help them grip the track as they push their sled at the start. The fastest recorded speed by a bobsleigh is 143km/h.

In the 2010 Winter Olympics the British racer Amy Williams reached this speed on her **skeleton** sled, winning a gold medal in a record-breaking 53.68 seconds.

Amy Williams winning gold at Vancouver in 2010

Fastest mammals

Which are the five fastest land animals in the world?

Cheetah: 113km/h
Pronghorn antelope: 98km/h
Wildebeest: 80km/h
Lion: 80km/h
Thomson's gazelle: 80km/h

How can a cheetah run so fast? Every part of its body is made for speed. Its body is slender and light, and its long tail helps it to stay balanced. Its claws grip the ground and help it to push forwards, just as a spiked track shoe helps a runner in a race.

From a standing start, a cheetah can **accelerate** to 96km/h in just three seconds. That is faster than most racing cars!

The spikes of running shoes work in the same way as a cheetah's claws.

Fastest birds

Which are the five fastest birds?

Peregrine falcon: 188–217km/h
White-throated needletail: 170km/h
Bewick's swan: 72km/h
Barnacle goose: 68km/h
Common crane: 68km/h

The peregrine falcon flies along at an impressive 188–217km/h. When it dives, it is faster still. It swoops down on its prey at amazing speeds of up to 390km/h.

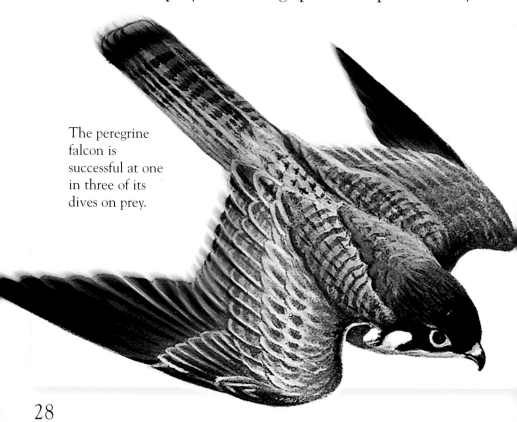

The peregrine falcon is successful at one in three of its dives on prey.

The common crane can fly across France in less than a day.

Scientists can find out how fast geese fly by fitting them with satellite transmitters.

Flying south for winter
Barnacle geese live in northern areas in summer. During the autumn they fly south to spend the winter somewhere warmer.

Fastest fish

Which are the five fastest fish?

Sailfish: 110km/h
Marlin: 80km/h
Wahoo: 78km/h
Southern bluefin tuna: 76km/h
Yellowfin tuna: 74km/h

A sailfish leaps out of the water if it is alarmed, raising its high fin like a sail to frighten its attackers or its prey.

When the sailfish is under the water, its fin is folded down, and the sailfish speeds along.

This striped marlin is hunting for sardines in the Pacific Ocean near Mexico.

The marlin swims fastest when it is deepest in the water, but it may still be eaten by a shark!

The bluefin tuna travels fast because its body is shaped like a missile.

Fastest dinosaurs

How fast did dinosaurs run?

Compsognathus: approx 65km/h
Velociraptor: approx 40km/h
Dilophosaurus: approx 40km/h
Allosaurus: approx 35km/h
Tyrannosaurus: approx 30km/h

How do we know how fast dinosaurs ran? People have found many dinosaur tracks and footprints. Scientists have used these tracks to work out approximately how fast the dinosaurs moved. These are some of the fastest.

Compsognathus was only the size of a chicken, but it was a super-fast dinosaur

Tyrannosaurus

Allosaurus

Dilophosaurus

Velociraptor

Did you know?
All the fastest dinosaurs were meat-eaters.
Their speed helped them to catch their prey.

33

Fastest in nature

Speeds in nature hardly change over time, unlike human speeds. People are always trying to go faster!

The fastest hummingbirds can beat their wings 90 times a second, allowing them to hover in one spot in the air while they drink nectar from flowers.

The fastest insect is the Australian dragonfly, which can fly at 58km/h.

The fastest-growing plant in the world is bamboo. It can grow 60 centimetres or more in a day.

The name hummingbird comes from the humming sound the bird's wings make while beating so fast.

This Venus flytrap is catching a dragonfly. These plants usually eat small insects such as flies and wasps.

The fastest killer in the plant world is the Venus flytrap, which can close on a mosquito in one fiftieth of a second!

The fastest flowing river in the world is the Atrato river in Colombia, South America. Every second, 4,900 cubic metres of water flow from the river into the Caribbean Sea.

Star performer
Comets fly at their fastest – 482km per second – when they are near the Sun, and they slow down as they move away. In 1843 one comet broke all records. It whisked right round the Sun in 2 hours, 7 minutes at a speed of 948km per second.

Fastest fingers, fastest brains

We humans can train our brains – and our fingers – to work incredibly fast.

A nine-year-old girl, Nandini Sankhla from India, once memorized a list of 100 objects in 9 minutes, 49 seconds. Afterwards, she could remember the list both in the order she learned it and backwards.

Txt it!
There are records for fastest texting. The test phrase for texting speed used by the *Guinness Book of World Records* is 160 characters long: *'The razor-toothed piranhas of the genera Serrasalmus and Pygocentrus are the most ferocious freshwater fish in the world. In reality they seldom attack a human.'* How fast can you text that? The world record is 34.65 seconds. It was set by Frode Ness in Oslo, Norway, in 2010.

The world record for solving the Rubik's cube is 5.66 seconds. It was set by Feliks Zemdegs of Australia in 2008.

Rubik record

In March 2010, 134 boys from a school in Amersham, UK, broke the record for the most people solving a Rubik's cube at once. They did it in 12 minutes.

Fastest sellers

The fastest-selling book ever is a book in the Harry Potter series. In the UK, an amazing 2,652,656 copies of the final title in the series, *Harry Potter and the Deathly Hallows*, were sold in the 24 hours after it came out.

Eager fans getting their copies of *Harry Potter and the Deathly Hallows*

Adult novels sell more slowly. Dan Brown's book *The Lost Symbol* sold a million copies in hardback and e-book versions in the US, the UK and Canada on its first day, making it the fastest-selling adult novel ever.

The fastest-selling DVD ever is *Avatar*, which sold 19.7 million copies in three weeks in 2010. This beat *The Dark Knight*, which sold 16 million copies in 2008.

Candle in the Wind sold so fast because it was released after Diana, Princess of Wales, died, and people bought it in memory of her.

The fastest-selling music single ever is Elton John's *Candle in the Wind*, which sold 1.55 million copies in its first week in 1997.

The fastest-selling download in Europe is Alexandra Burke's version of Leonard Cohen's song *Hallelujah*. More than 105,000 copies of the song were sold on the day after she won the UK TV singing competition *The X Factor* in 2008.

Burke became the first British female soloist to sell one million copies of a single in the UK.

More and more people!

The fastest growing cities in the world between 2000 and 2010 were all in Asia and Africa.

During these ten years, the number of people living in Guangzhou in China grew by 3.3 million. The number of people living in Karachi in Pakistan grew by 3.1 million and the number of people living in Delhi in India by 2.9 million.

Guangzhou is a busy, fast-growing city.
It has many thriving industries.

The old street market in Delhi teems with people.

Today, these three cities are the fastest-growing in the world.

City	3m	6m	9m	12m	15m
Guangzhou					
Karachi					
Delhi					

Millions of people in 2000	
Millions of people in 2010	

How many people altogether?

At the start of 2012 there were about 7,000,000 (seven billion) people in the world. Experts think that this will grow to well over nine billion by 2050.

Crazy speed records

Here are some crazy speed records.

Ashrita Furman broke his own world record for pushing an orange with his nose in New York, USA, in 2007. His new record was a mile in 22 minutes, 41 seconds.

Ashrita Furman has set 356 official world records since 1979. Here he is pushing an orange with his nose.

Erick Hernandez from Cuba broke the world record for football ball control in October 2009. He touched the ball 341 times with his head in 60 seconds.

'Flying Phil' Rabinowitz, who kept fit by walking 6km every day

South African Philip Rabinowitz tried to set a record as the fastest 100-year-old to run 100 metres, in Cape Town, South Africa, in July 2004. He failed in his bid because a power cut stopped the electronic clocks.

Metin Senturk is a blind Turkish singer who set a world record for driving a car when blind and unaccompanied in April 2010. He reached a speed of 292.89km/h in a Ferrari F430 car.

Senturk was guided by a person in a vehicle behind him, giving instructions through an earpiece.

Or why not slow down?

Let's take a break, and celebrate some of the slowest things on Earth.

A crocodile can slow down its heart so that it beats just twice a minute. This lets the crocodile hold its breath for as long as an hour when it is under water.

A sloth moves so slowly that algae grows on its furry coat.

A seahorse rarely travels faster than 0.016km/h.

A British fund raiser, Lloyd Scott, set a world record for the slowest marathon in Edinburgh, Scotland, in 2003. He wore a deep-sea diving suit and he took 6 days, 4 hours, 30 minutes, 56 seconds to cover the distance.

Snail mail
Ethel Martin of Oberlin, Kansas, USA, received the slowest-ever Christmas card. It took 93 years to reach her. Her cousins in Nebraska posted the card on 23 December 1914 and it finally arrived in December 2007!

Glossary

accelerate To go faster.

aerodynamic An aerodynamic shape lets air flow easily past an object so it can move faster through the air.

atmosphere The layer of gases immediately above the Earth's surface.

automobile The early name for a motor car.

carbon fibre A material that is very light in weight and very strong, so is good for making boats, bicycles and bobsleighs.

clipper ship A fast sailing ship in the nineteenth century which could 'clip' or cut through the waves.

free-falling Falling through the sky without a parachute.

freestyle In swimming, freestyle means any stroke. Swimmers usually choose front crawl for a freestyle race, because it's the fastest stroke.

friction The force that slows things down and stops them moving.

Grand Prix (plural: Grands Prix) The French term for big prize. A Formula One motor race is known as a Grand Prix.

hydroplane A motorboat that races just above the surface of the water.

internal combustion engine An engine that is driven by burning petrol or diesel with air.

jet engine A very fast internal combustion engine, which works by moving a jet of liquid.

penny farthing A bicycle invented in 1871. It was nicknamed the penny farthing because of the size of its wheels – a penny was a large coin and a farthing was a small coin. The large front wheel helped it go faster and ride over rough surfaces.

recumbent A lying down position.

revs Short for revolutions, the number of times an engine turns over (or revolves) every minute.

skeleton Tobogganing face downwards on a small, light sled; there are no brakes!

solo One person on their own.

sound barrier The point at which an vehicle goes faster than the sound it makes, and so becomes supersonic.

steam power Force or energy produced by heating water.

suspension The springs and shock absorbers in a car or bicycle.

TGV The French *train à grande vitesse*, which means high speed train.

wind resistance The force, or drag, of the wind slowing down a moving object. If a vehicle has an aerodynamic shape it cuts down its wind resistance.

Index